RAISING CHILDREN
WITHOUT FEAR

Kenneth & Gloria COPELAND

Unless otherwise noted, all scripture is from the *King James Version* of the Bible.

Scripture quotations marked *The Amplified Bible* are from *The Amplified Bible, Old Testament* © 1965, 1987 by The Zondervan Corporation. *The Amplified New Testament* © 1958, 1987 by The Lockman Foundation. Used by permission.

Raising Children Without Fear

ISBN 1-57562-742-6   30-0733

08 07 06 05 04 03   6 5 4 3 2 1

©2002 Eagle Mountain International Church, Incorporated aka Kenneth Copeland Ministries

Kenneth Copeland Publications
Fort Worth, Texas 76192-0001

For more information about Kenneth Copeland Ministries, call 1-800-600-7395 or visit www.kcm.org.

Printed in the United States of America. All rights reserved under International Copyright Law. No part of this book may be reproduced or transmitted in any form or by any means, electronic or mechanical, including photocopying, recording, or by any information storage and retrieval system, without the written permission of the publisher.

On the cover: Courtney Copeland, at the age of 2, with father, John Copeland, in the background.

"Train up a child in the way he should go: and when he is old, he will not depart from it" (Proverbs 22:6).

Raising Children in Perverse Times

by Gloria Copeland

Your children are precious to you. The Scripture calls them a heritage and a reward. You love them so much that you want them to grow and mature into happy, healthy, successful adults. But do you love them enough to train them the way God says in His Word, to be an example to them and even to correct them?

If you are a parent, God has commanded you to teach and train your children in His

Word and His ways so that they can live a victorious life. It's not an option. It's a responsibility that each of us as parents will have to answer for.

Genesis 18:19 indicates that God chose Abraham because He knew Abraham would teach his children to keep the ways of the Lord. It's evident this is very important to God.

> *God chose Abraham because He knew Abraham would teach his children to keep the ways of the Lord.*

We live in a time when the world is getting darker and it is becoming more of a challenge to live holy. Even those who are saved can find themselves bombarded with all kinds of ungodly, perverse sights and sounds from television, movies, magazines, the Internet—you name it. If adults are being challenged with negative input and temptation, just think what kind of environment today's children are growing up in. If they don't have strong parental direction and training, the enemy is sure to have free reign in their lives. Taking your place as a godly parent has never been more important.

> *Taking your place as a godly parent has never been more important.*

The enemy wants to control the lives of as many people as he can. He does this by tricking them into going his way. He is peddling murder, hate and every kind of ungodly, immoral thing you can think of. If he can get those kinds of things before a person's eyes and in their ears, he will have a place in their life.

Unfortunately, even some Christians are opening the door to the enemy by taking part in the world's unclean entertainment and activities. They may think it won't hurt them, but people can't feed on the world's trash and not be affected.

If we don't fight the good fight of faith (1 Timothy 6:12), the devil will come in and take over our homes and our children. And remember, when he comes in, he brings the curse with him. We must fight to keep our homes devil free!

Be Ye Separate

Do you realize that consistently living a holy lifestyle has everything to do with how your children turn out? If you go to church and talk right and look good in front of people, but then you live differently at home, you are making it very hard for your children to take God seriously. As they are growing up, children learn more by watching what you do than by listening to what you say. And they never forget what they observe at home.

> *Children learn more by watching what you do than by listening to what you say.*

Holiness is letting God separate you out of the darkness of the world into a life that is worth living—a life lived in Him.

Be ye not unequally yoked together with unbelievers: for what fellowship hath righteousness with unrighteousness? and what communion hath light with darkness?...or what part hath he that believeth with an infidel? And what agreement hath the temple of God with idols? for ye are the temple of the living God; as God hath said, I will dwell in them, and walk in them....Wherefore come out from among them, and be ye separate, saith the Lord, and touch not the unclean thing... (2 Corinthians 6:14-17).

The word *separate* means "to set apart, to disunite, to divide, to part company, to go in a different direction, to cease to be associated with, to become distinct or disengaged, as cream separates from milk."

So to get a picture of how we're to live, think about how cream rises to the top and is separated from the plain milk.

That's exactly what we have to do in regard to the sin the world is endeavoring to sell us on every hand. We must rise above it by doing what Romans 12:2 says: "Be not conformed to this world: but be ye transformed by the renewing of your mind...."

When Ken and I got born again and filled with the Spirit, God pulled us out of darkness. But our lives didn't change much until the Word began to wash our minds (Ephesians 5:26) and we began to understand that things like sin, sickness and poverty did not belong to us anymore. Then we began to resist those things.

However, if someone decided to stay in the darkness and live against the Word, then he would be living in sin. That would be very dangerous because it shows a lack of reverence—or fear—for God. And the fear of God is what brings us so many promises. Without it people won't experience the protection they could have, and neither will their families.

We're not just choosing for our own lives when we make choices. Deuteronomy 30:19 says, "I have set before you life and death, blessing and cursing: therefore choose life, that both thou and thy seed may live." The decisions we make not only affect us—they also affect our children.

You're Not What You Used to Be

If you are a Christian, the wicked ways of the world should be a thing of the past. First Peter 4:3 in *The Amplified Bible* pretty well sums it up: "For the time that is past already suffices for doing what the Gentiles like to do—living [as you have done] in shameless, insolent wantonness, in lustful desires, drunkenness, reveling, drinking bouts and abominable, lawless idolatries."

Many people have become arrogant about sin. They think, *I'll just do this for a while. God will forgive me.* If you are truly repentant, yes, God will forgive you, but what kind of confusion will you create in the meantime for yourself and your family? Another thing to remember is that by continually yielding to sin, you can become so entangled in it that you no longer have the will to repent. Consider Hebrews 6:4-9:

> For it is impossible [to restore and bring again to repentance] those who have been once for all enlightened, who have consciously tasted the heavenly gift and have become sharers of the Holy Spirit. And have felt how good the Word of God is and the mighty powers of the age and world to come, if they then deviate from the faith and turn away from their allegiance—[it is impossible] to bring them back to repentance, for (because, while, as long as) they nail upon the cross the Son of God afresh [as far as they are concerned] and are holding [Him] up to contempt and

shame and public disgrace. For the soil which has drunk the rain that repeatedly falls upon it and produces vegetation useful to those for whose benefit it is cultivated partakes of a blessing from God. But if [that same soil] persistently bears thorns and thistles, it is considered worthless and near to being cursed, whose end is to be burned. [Gen. 3:17, 18.] Even though we speak this way, yet in your case, beloved, we are now firmly convinced of better things that are near to salvation and accompany it (*The Amplified Bible*).

Think soberly about what you are doing. If you are entertaining sin, please think about the consequences of your actions and what it will do to your children.

This scripture didn't say God wouldn't forgive those who had been enlightened and were now entangled but those who would not repent. Hopefully you will realize, *There's no way I'm going to tear my family up by committing adultery or any other rebellion against God.*

Titus 2:11-12 says, "For the grace of God that bringeth salvation hath appeared to all men, teaching us that, denying ungodliness and worldly lusts, we should live soberly, righteously, and godly, in this present world."

Here is the bottom line: "But as the One Who called you is holy, you yourselves also be holy in all your conduct and manner of living" (1 Peter 1:15, *The Amplified Bible*). Verses 18-19 go on to make these powerful statements: "You must know (recognize) that you were redeemed (ransomed) from the useless (fruitless) way of living inherited by tradition from [your] forefathers, not with corruptible things [such as] silver and gold, But [you were purchased] with the precious blood of Christ (the Messiah), like that of a [sacrificial] lamb without blemish or spot."

You may have inherited a fruitless way of living, but you can be the one to stop that cycle in your family. You are no longer your own. You were purchased with the precious blood of Jesus. It separates you and makes you righteous and holy. Teach *that* to your children. Let *that* be the legacy you pass on to them.

> *You may have inherited a fruitless way of living, but you can be the one to stop that cycle in your family.*

Teach Your Children What God Says

If God wants you to be separated, how much more important is it for your children to be separated from the vile things of the world? Little children are being taught from elementary school that homosexuality is OK—it's an alternative lifestyle. They are being taught that they can choose to do whatever makes them happy. Generations of children are growing up without God in their lives, without boundaries. They have no Ten Commandments to live by, no basis for morality.

But it doesn't have to be that way in your family—and it shouldn't be. Over and over the Bible commands parents to teach their children the Word of God (Deuteronomy 6:6-7, 11:18-21). That will make all the difference in what kind of people they grow up to be.

If you fail to teach your children what God's Word says is moral or immoral, you can be sure the world will teach them what it believes. Your children may come home with a book that talks about "Heather has two mommies," and they should already know what the Bible says about this issue and why it is wrong. If you haven't already discussed homosexuality with them, take time to do so. If your children attend public school, you may have to deal with it earlier than you would choose. Watch carefully what others are depositing in your children. Talk to their teachers. Ask them what materials they use. Talk to your children and monitor what they are hearing and seeing.

In Leviticus 18, God deals with homosexuality and other sexual sins. He also makes it plain that His people are not to mingle among the heathen and learn their ways.

First Corinthians 15:33 adds, "Do not be so deceived and misled! Evil companionships (communion, associations) corrupt and deprave good manners and morals and character" (*The Amplified Bible*).

And James 4:4 goes on to say, "Whosoever therefore will be a friend of the world is the enemy of God."

These are important lessons to teach your children, considering the kind of peer pressure they are sure to experience in today's world.

It's also important to train your children to walk with God on a daily basis by reading the Word, praying and spending time with Him. Teach them to desire spiritual things and help them learn to "walk in the Spirit, and [they] shall not fulfil the lust of the flesh" (Galatians 5:16).

Certainly, I haven't covered everything

you should teach your children from the Word. There's so much more. But remember this: Your victory is tied up in your obedience. Obeying God's Word and teaching your children to do the same will ensure the future of your family.

> *Your victory is tied up in your obedience. Obeying God's Word and teaching your children to do the same will ensure the future of your family.*

When you choose a church, think about your children as well as yourself. There are many good churches with excellent children's training. Get your children involved in these programs.

Most of all, be mindful that living a godly life before your children is the best teacher! So provide a solid home with love and support, and show them by example how to live separated unto God. Let them see how you respond when bad news or trouble comes. Let them see your faith in action. Let them see how you handle all kinds of circumstances—they will never escape that influence.

They might forget your words, but they won't forget your ways.

Promises for Children

"And all thy children shall be taught of the Lord; and great shall be the peace of thy children" (Isaiah 54:13).

"Hear, ye children, the instruction of a father, and attend to know understanding" (Proverbs 4:1).

"My son, keep thy father's commandment, and forsake not the law of thy mother: Bind them continually upon thine heart, and tie them about thy neck. When thou goest, it shall lead thee...and when thou *awakest, it shall talk with thee"* (Proverbs 6:20, 22).

"A wise son heareth his father's instruction" (Proverbs 13:1).

"A fool despiseth his father's instruction: but he that regardeth reproof is prudent" (Proverbs 15:5).

"Whoso keepeth the law is a wise son: but he that is a companion of riotous men shameth his father" (Proverbs 28:7).

"Children, obey your parents in the Lord: for this is right. Honour thy father and mother;

which is the first commandment with promise; that it may be well with thee, and thou mayest live long on the earth"
(Ephesians 6:1-3).

"Children, obey your parents in all things: for this is well pleasing unto the Lord"
(Colossians 3:20).

"Flee also youthful lusts: but follow righteousness, faith, charity, peace, with them that call on the Lord out of a pure heart"
(2 Timothy 2:22).

Raising Children Without Fear

by Kenneth Copeland

A number of years ago, singer and songwriter Johnny Cash recorded the song, "A Boy Named Sue." While this song is meant to be lighthearted and humorous, it also speaks volumes about how parents can fall into the trap of trying to control and manipulate their children.

In this particular song, a rough-and-tough father who is about to abandon his family decides to name his son *Sue* in an effort to toughen him up and cause him to become a "real man."

As expected, the boy ends up fighting his way through life because of the shame of having a girl's name.

While this father's plan did make his son tough, it did not build strong character in him. Beating the daylights out of everyone who crosses you doesn't make you strong.

The strongest men are not men of violence. They are men who know how to love with the love of God.

It Worked for Mama...
Or Did It?

In the same way the father in "A Boy Named Sue" used shame and humiliation to toughen up his son, parents today—like countless generations of parents before them—have used *fear* to try and change or control the behavior of their children.

For instance, how many times have you heard or said something like this: "Now, sweetheart, don't run out in the street like that again. Daddy is afraid you will get hit by a car."

That's fear—pure and simple. It is using fear to manipulate your child into doing what you want him or her to do. What's more, by saying those kinds of things you are raising your child in a spirit of fear.

"Oh, but Brother Copeland, how else is a child going to learn to watch out for cars and be safe? Everyone knows in a situation like this that a little fear might be healthy."

That's a lie from the devil. There is *never* a time when a little fear—or a lot for that matter—is healthy.

Revelation 21:8 exposes the deception in that kind of thinking: "But the fearful, and unbelieving, and the abominable, and murderers, and whoremongers, and sorcerers, and idolaters, and all liars, shall have their part in the lake which burneth with fire and brimstone: which is the second death."

Fear, doubt, abominations, murder, whoremongering, sorcery, idolatry, lying—not one of these is healthy. Not in the slightest.

And notice where *fear* is on this list of undesirables—at the very top.

The truth is, you really have no desire for your children to be afraid, or *fear-full*. No parent does. You wouldn't have your children terrorized every time they see a car coming. You simply would like for them to develop enough sound judgment about cars to stay out of the street and not get hit.

But parents often fall back on fear to try and get the job done.

Why?

Because that's the way their parents raised them, which was how their parents raised them and how their parents raised them.

Out of ignorance, generation after generation has sown fear into its children. And generation after generation has reaped that fear.

Now granted, children do need information to help them succeed in life. But they also need to be taught how to walk by faith—and not just in potentially dangerous situations, such as getting hit by a car. They need to be shown how to take the Word of God and use it to meet any situation head-on and overcome it—not run from it.

When Parents Get Out of Control

To break a cycle of fear in your life and the lives of your children, you need to go first to the Lord and ask Him if you are indeed promoting and imparting a spirit of fear to your children. If you are, repent of it before God. It's not your job to control and change people anyway—not even your own children. And you certainly should not be trying to do it through fear.

We are reminded in 2 Timothy 1:7 that "God hath not given us the spirit of fear; but of power, and of love, and of a sound mind."

Since God did not give us a spirit of fear, we have no business promoting it or using it as a tool, especially where our children are concerned.

If your children are going to have sound judgment and sound decision-making skills, then you must take time to teach them. You are going to have to invest quality time in them. One of the reasons there's been so much failure in raising children is because parents are not taking the time to love them through prayer. By that I mean setting aside a designated time to pray for them and hold them before the Lord.

Now I'm not talking about crying out, "Oh God, can't You help me with these kids? I'm afraid they're going to jail. I just know they're doing drugs."

No, that's fear-based prayer. It's praying out of torment. And the only results it will get you are disastrous. That kind of praying will connect you to the terrible things you are afraid of.

The kind of prayer I'm talking about is moments of quietness when you call the names of your children before God and purposely begin to love them from your heart with "the love of God [that] is shed abroad in our hearts by the Holy Ghost..." (Romans 5:5). Through prayer, bathe them in faith and love—after all faith works by love (Galatians 5:6).

So instead of fretful, tormented prayers, pray something like this: "Lord, I love my son and I'm holding him before You right now. I see You holding him in Your arms, ministering life, peace and comfort to him. Lord, I realize that You love him far more than I ever could. And Father, I pray for the peace of God that passes all understanding to stand guard over his heart and mind. Help him, Lord, to be full of You, to know You, and to worship You. And Father, help me see my son the way You see him. Help me love him with Your love."

As a word of caution, when you begin praying this way, it may seem a little shallow at first. But remember, love at its most shallow point is deeper than anything else.

If you desire to see your children develop strong godly character, love them with the love that He has imparted to your heart as a parent. And realize that His love is not merely human love, it's supernatural Love—Himself.

Allow that love to grow, expand and develop until you become rooted and grounded in love, that you might be filled with all the fullness of God (Ephesians 3:17-19).

Once you are filled with the fullness of God, there is no room for fear. Every prayer you pray for your children...every thought of them...will be love-based and faith-based.

And love never fails.

Prayer for Salvation and Baptism in the Holy Spirit

Heavenly Father, I come to You in the Name of Jesus. Your Word says, "Whosoever shall call on the name of the Lord shall be saved" (Acts 2:21). I am calling on You. I pray and ask Jesus to come into my heart and be Lord over my life according to Romans 10:9-10: "If thou shalt confess with thy mouth the Lord Jesus, and shalt believe in thine heart that God hath raised him from the dead, thou shalt be saved. For with the heart man believeth unto righteousness; and with the mouth confession is made unto salvation." I do that now. I confess that Jesus is Lord, and I believe in my heart that God raised Him from the dead.

I am now reborn! I am a Christian—a child of Almighty God! I am saved! You also said in Your Word, "If ye then, being evil, know how to give good gifts unto your children: HOW MUCH MORE shall your heavenly Father give the Holy Spirit to them that ask him?" (Luke 11:13). I'm also asking You to fill me with the Holy Spirit. Holy Spirit, rise up within me as I praise God. I fully expect to speak with other tongues as You give me the utterance (Acts 2:4). In Jesus' Name. Amen!

Begin to praise God for filling you with the Holy Spirit. Speak those words and syllables you receive—not in your own language, but the language given to you by the Holy Spirit. You have to use your own voice. God will not force you to speak. Don't be concerned with how it sounds. It is a heavenly language!

Continue with the blessing God has given you and pray in the spirit every day.

You are a born-again, Spirit-filled believer. You'll never be the same!

Find a good church that boldly preaches God's Word and obeys it. Become a part of a church family who will love and care for you as you love and care for them.

We need to be connected to each other. It increases our strength in God. It's God's plan for us.

Make it a habit to watch the *Believer's Voice of Victory* television broadcast and become a doer of the Word, who is blessed in his doing (James 1:22-25).

About the Authors

Kenneth and Gloria Copeland are the best-selling authors of more than sixty books such as the popular *Living Contact* and *Managing God's Mutual Funds—Yours and His*. They have co-authored numerous other books including *Family Promises* and *From Faith to Faith—A Daily Guide to Victory*. As founders of Kenneth Copeland Ministries in Fort Worth, Texas, Kenneth and Gloria are in their 36th year of circling the globe with the uncompromised Word of God, preaching and teaching a lifestyle of victory for every Christian.

Their daily and Sunday *Believer's Voice of Victory* television broadcasts now air on more than 500 stations around the world, and their *Believer's Voice of Victory* and *Shout!* magazines are distributed to more than one million adults and children worldwide. Their international prison ministry reaches an average of 60,000 new inmates every year and receives more than 17,000 pieces of correspondence each month. Their teaching materials can also be found on the World Wide Web. With offices and staff in the United States, Canada, England, Australia, South Africa and Ukraine, Kenneth and Gloria's teaching materials—books, magazines, audios and videos—have been translated into at least twenty-two languages to reach the world with the love of God.

Learn more about
Kenneth Copeland Ministries
by visiting our Web site
at **www.kcm.org**

Materials to Help You Receive Your Healing by Gloria Copeland

Books

* And Jesus Healed Them All
  God's Prescription for Divine Health
* Harvest of Health
  Words That Heal
  (gift book with CD enclosed)

Audio Resources

God Is a Good God
God Wants You Well
Healing School

Video Resources

Healing School: God Wants You Well
Know Him as Healer

Books Available From Kenneth Copeland Ministries

by Kenneth Copeland

*   A Ceremony of Marriage
       A Matter of Choice
       Covenant of Blood
       Faith and Patience—The Power Twins
*   Freedom From Fear
       Giving and Receiving
       Honor—Walking in Honesty, Truth and Integrity
       How to Conquer Strife
       How to Discipline Your Flesh
       How to Receive Communion
       In Love There Is No Fear
       Know Your Enemy
       Living at the End of Time—A Time of Supernatural Increase
       Love Never Fails
       Managing God's Mutual Funds—Yours and His
       Mercy—The Divine Rescue of the Human Race
*   Now Are We in Christ Jesus
       One Nation Under God (gift book with CD enclosed)
*   Our Covenant With God

- Partnership, Sharing the Vision—Sharing the Grace
- *Prayer—Your Foundation for Success
- *Prosperity: The Choice Is Yours
- Rumors of War
- *Sensitivity of Heart
- *Six Steps to Excellence in Ministry
- *Sorrow Not! Winning Over Grief and Sorrow
- *The Decision Is Yours
- *The Force of Faith
- *The Force of Righteousness
- The Image of God in You
- *The Laws of Prosperity
- *The Mercy of God (available in Spanish only)
- The Outpouring of the Spirit—The Result of Prayer
- *The Power of the Tongue
- The Power to Be Forever Free
- *The Winning Attitude
- Turn Your Hurts Into Harvests
- Walking in the Realm of the Miraculous
- *Welcome to the Family
- *You Are Healed!
- Your Right-Standing With God

*Available in Spanish

by Gloria Copeland

- * And Jesus Healed Them All
- Are You Listening?
- Are You Ready?
- Be a Vessel of Honor
- Build Your Financial Foundation
- Fight On!
- Go With the Flow
- God's Prescription for Divine Health
- God's Success Formula
- God's Will for You
- God's Will for Your Healing
- God's Will Is Prosperity
- * God's Will Is the Holy Spirit
- * Harvest of Health
- Hidden Treasures
- Living Contact
- Living in Heaven's Blessings Now
- Looking for a Receiver
- * Love—The Secret to Your Success
- No Deposit—No Return
- Pleasing the Father
- Pressing In—It's Worth It All
- Shine On!
- The Grace That Makes Us Holy
- The Power to Live a New Life
- The Protection of Angels
- There Is No High Like the Most High

The Secret Place of God's
  Protection (gift book with CD enclosed)
The Unbeatable Spirit of Faith
This Same Jesus
To Know Him
* Walk in the Spirit (available in Spanish only)
Walk With God
Well Worth the Wait
Words That Heal (gift book with CD enclosed)
Your Promise of Protection—The
  Power of the 91st Psalm

Books Co-Authored by Kenneth and Gloria Copeland

Family Promises
Healing Promises
Prosperity Promises
Protection Promises

* From Faith to Faith—A Daily
  Guide to Victory
From Faith to Faith—A Perpetual
  Calendar

One Word From God Can Change Your Life

One Word From God Series:
• One Word From God Can Change Your
  Destiny

*Available in Spanish

- One Word From God Can Change Your Family
- One Word From God Can Change Your Finances
- One Word From God Can Change Your Formula for Success
- One Word From God Can Change Your Health
- One Word From God Can Change Your Nation
- One Word From God Can Change Your Prayer Life
- One Word From God Can Change Your Relationships

Load Up—A Youth Devotional
Over the Edge—A Youth Devotional
Pursuit of His Presence—A Daily Devotional
Pursuit of His Presence—A Perpetual Calendar

Other Books Published by KCP

The First 30 Years—A Journey of Faith
 The story of the lives of Kenneth and Gloria Copeland
Real People. Real Needs. Real Victories.
 A book of testimonies to encourage your faith

John G. Lake—His Life, His Sermons, His Boldness of Faith
The Holiest of All by Andrew Murray
The New Testament in Modern Speech by Richard Francis Weymouth
The Rabbi From Burbank by Rabbi Isidor Zwirn and Bob Owen
Unchained by Mac Gober

Products Designed for Today's Children and Youth

And Jesus Healed Them All (confession book and CD gift package)
Baby Praise Board Book
Baby Praise Christmas Board Book
Noah's Ark Coloring Book
The Best of *Shout!* Adventure Comics
The *Shout!* Giant Flip Coloring Book
The *Shout!* Joke Book
The *Shout!* Super-Activity Book
Wichita Slim's Campfire Stories

*Commander Kellie and the Superkids*_{SM} Books:

The SWORD Adventure Book
*Commander Kellie and the Superkids*_{SM} Solve-It-Yourself Mysteries

*Commander Kellie and the Superkids*_{SM} Adventure Series:
Middle Grade Novels by Christopher P.N. Maselli:

#1 The Mysterious Presence
#2 The Quest for the Second Half
#3 Escape From Jungle Island
#4 In Pursuit of the Enemy
#5 Caged Rivalry
#6 Mystery of the Missing Junk
#7 Out of Breath
#8 The Year Mashela Stole Christmas
#9 False Identity

World Offices of Kenneth Copeland Ministries

For more information about KCM and a free catalog, please write the office nearest you:

Kenneth Copeland Ministries
Fort Worth, Texas 76192-0001

Kenneth Copeland
Locked Bag 2600
Mansfield Delivery Centre
QUEENSLAND 4122
AUSTRALIA

Kenneth Copeland
Post Office Box 15
BATH
BA1 3XN
U.K.

Kenneth Copeland
Private Bag X 909
FONTAINEBLEAU
2032
REPUBLIC OF
SOUTH AFRICA

Kenneth Copeland
Post Office Box 378
Surrey, B.C.
V3T 5B6
CANADA

Kenneth Copeland Ministries
Post Office Box 84
L'VIV 79000
UKRAINE

We're Here for You!

Believer's Voice of Victory Television Broadcast

Join Kenneth and Gloria Copeland and the *Believer's Voice of Victory* broadcasts Monday through Friday and on Sunday each week, and learn how faith in God's Word can take your life from ordinary to extraordinary. This teaching from God's Word is designed to get you where you want to be—*on top!*

You can catch the *Believer's Voice of Victory* broadcast on your local, cable or satellite channels.

Check your local listings for times and stations in your area.

Believer's Voice of Victory Magazine

Enjoy inspired teaching and encouragement from Kenneth and Gloria Copeland and guest ministers each month in the *Believer's Voice of Victory* magazine. Also included are real-life testimonies of God's miraculous power and divine intervention in the lives of people just like you!

It's more than just a magazine—it's a ministry.

To receive a FREE subscription to *Believer's Voice of Victory*, write to:

Kenneth Copeland Ministries
Fort Worth, Texas 76192-0001

Or call:
1-800-600-7395
(7 a.m.-5 p.m. CT)
Or visit our Web site at:
www.kcm.org

If you are writing from outside the U.S., please contact the KCM office nearest you. Addresses for all Kenneth Copeland Ministries offices are listed on the previous pages.